MIJIKENDA

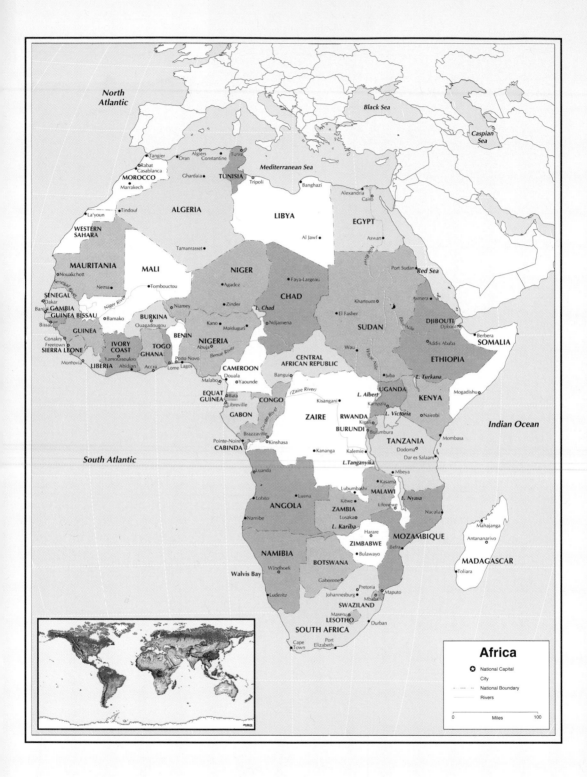

Africa

North
Atlantic

Black Sea

Caspian
Sea

MOROCCO
Tangier
Rabat
Casablanca
Marrakech
La'youn
Tindouf
Oran
Algiers
Constantine
Tunis

WESTERN
SAHARA

Ghardaia

TUNISIA
Tripoli

Mediterranean Sea

Banghazi

Alexandria
Cairo

ALGERIA

LIBYA

EGYPT

MAURITANIA
Nouakchott
Nema

MALI
Tamanrasset

Al Jawf

Aswan

Port Sudan
Red Sea

Senegal River
SENEGAL
Dakar
Banjul
GAMBIA
GUINEA BISSAU
Bissau
Conakry
Freetown
SIERRA LEONE
Montrovia
LIBERIA

Niger River
Tombouctou

NIGER
Agadez

Zinder

L. Chad

CHAD

Faya-Largeau

Khartoum
El Fasher

SUDAN

Asmera

Blue Nile

DJIBOUTI
Djibouti
Berbera

Bamako
BURKINA
Ouagadougou
Kano
Maiduguri
Niamey

Ndjamena

Wau

White Nile

Addis Ababa
ETHIOPIA

SOMALIA

GUINEA
IVORY
COAST
TOGO
GHANA
Abidjan
Accra
BENIN
NIGERIA
Abuja
Benue River
Porto Novo
Lome Lagos

CAMEROON
Douala
Yaounde
Malabo

CENTRAL
AFRICAN REPUBLIC
Bangui

Juba

L. Turkana

UGANDA
Kampala

Mogadishu

KENYA

EQUAT.
GUINEA
Bata
Libreville
GABON

CONGO

Congo River
(Zaire River)
Kisangani

L. Albert

Nairobi

Indian Ocean

Brazzaville
Pointe-Noire
CABINDA
Kinshasa

ZAIRE

RWANDA
Kigali
BURUNDI
Bujumbura
L. Victoria

TANZANIA
Dodoma
Dar es Salaam
Mombasa

Kanana

Kalemie

South Atlantic

Luanda

L.Tanganyika

Mbeya

Lobito
Lucna
ANGOLA
Namibe

Lubumbashi
Kitwe
ZAMBIA
Lusaka
L. Kariba

Kasama
MALAWI
Lilongwe
L. Nyasa
Nacala

MOZAMBIQUE

NAMIBIA
Windhoek
Walvis Bay
Luderitz

BOTSWANA
Gaborone

Harare
ZIMBABWE
Bulawayo
Befra

Mahajanga
Antananarivo

MADAGASCAR
Toliara

Johannesburg
Pretoria
Mbabane
Maputo
SWAZILAND
Maseru
LESOTHO
Durban
SOUTH AFRICA
Cape
Town
Port
Elizabeth

Africa

⊕ National Capital
∘ City
- - - National Boundary
—— Rivers

0   Miles   100

The Heritage Library of African Peoples

MIJIKENDA

Tiyambe Zeleza, Ph.D.

THE ROSEN PUBLISHING GROUP, INC.
NEW YORK

Published in 1995 by The Rosen Publishing Group, Inc.
29 East 21st Street, New York, NY 10010

First Edition

Library of Congress Cataloging-in-Publication Data

Zeleza, Tiyambe, 1955–
    Mijikenda / Tiyambe Zeleza.—1st ed.
        p.   cm.—(The Heritage library of African peoples)
    Includes bibliographical references and index.
    ISBN 0–8239–1767–3
    1. Nika (African people)—History—Juvenile literature.   2. Nika
(African people)—Social life and customs—Juvenile literature.
I. Title.   II. Series.
DT433.545.N55Z45   1995   95-25657
960′.0496395—dc20   CIP
                                                              AC

Manufactured in the United States of America

Contents

1. Origins of the Mijikenda   9

2. Before and After the *Kaya*   15

3. Customs and Ritual   23

4. The European Conquest   27

5. Changes Caused by Colonial Rule   35

6. The Mijikenda and Independence   42

7. Changes Now and into the Future   46

Conclusion   56

Glossary   58

For Further Reading   59

Index   61

INTRODUCTION

THERE IS EVERY REASON FOR US TO KNOW something about Africa and to understand its past and the way of life of its peoples. Africa is a rich continent that has for centuries provided the world with art, culture, labor, wealth, and natural resources. It has vast mineral deposits, fossil fuels, and commercial crops.

But perhaps most important is the fact that fossil evidence indicates that human beings originated in Africa. The earliest traces of human beings and their tools are almost two million years old. Their descendants have migrated throughout the world. To be human is to be of African descent.

The experiences of the peoples who stayed in Africa are as rich and as diverse as of those who established themselves elsewhere. This series of books describes their environment, relationships, and their customs and beliefs. The books present the variety of languages, histories, cultures, and religions that are to be found on the African continent. They demonstrate the historical linkages between African peoples and the way contemporary Africa has been affected by European colonial rule.

Africa is large, complex, and diverse. It encompasses an area of more than 11,700,000

square miles. The United States, Europe, and India could fit easily into it. The sheer size is an indication of the continent's great variety in geography, terrain, climate, flora, fauna, peoples, languages, and cultures.

Much of contemporary Africa has been shaped by European colonial rule, industrialization, urbanization, and the demands of a world economic system. For more than seventy years, large regions of Africa were ruled by Great Britain, France, Belgium, Portugal, and Spain. African peoples from various ethnic, linguistic, and cultural backgrounds were brought together to form colonial states.

For decades Africans struggled to gain their independence. It was not until after World War II that the colonial territories became independent African states. Today, almost all of Africa is ruled by Africans. Large numbers of Africans live in modern cities. Rural Africa is also being transformed, and yet its people still engage in many of their age-old customs and beliefs.

Contemporary circumstances and natural events have not always been kind to ordinary Africans. Today, however, new social movements and technological innovations pose great promise for future development.

George Bond
Institute of African Studies
Columbia University, New York City

The Mijikenda live on the coast of Kenya.

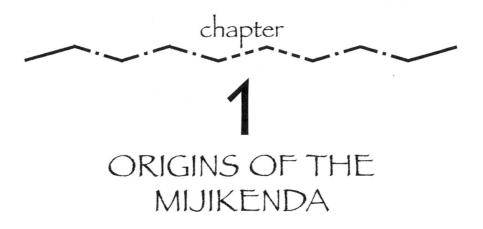

chapter

1

ORIGINS OF THE MIJIKENDA

THE MIJIKENDA CURRENTLY NUMBER OVER 750,000 people, the most numerous group in the coastal region of Kenya. They comprise nine peoples who have separate cultures but are very similar. The Mijikenda peoples are, from north to south, the Giriama, Kauma, Chonyi, Jibana, Kambe, Ribe, Rabai, Duruma, and Digo. The Giriama, who live on the Sabaki River, make up about half of the entire Mijikenda population. The Digo live farthest south, on the Kenya-Tanzania border.

The name *Mijikenda* means "the nine villages." It was adopted in the 1940s. Before that the peoples were known as the Nyika (or Nika), meaning "bush people," which they found insulting.

All the Mijikenda languages are part of the Sabaki group in the Bantu language family. The

A rural Mijikenda woman transporting water from a well to the village.

Sabaki group also includes the languages of Swahili and Pokomo.

The ancestors of the Mijikenda, Pokomo, and Swahili lived in Somalia until the tenth century, when the Swahili began to move down the coast. The others began migrating from Somalia into Kenya in the mid-sixteenth century. The Pokomo settled along the Tana River, and the many Mijikenda groups spread farther south.

A GIRIAMA ORIGIN MYTH

Muyeye was the name of the first Giriama man. He had two wives. Their names were Mbodze and Matsezi. Muyeye's two wives had children, and they were the first Mijikenda. They lived in Singwaya near the Oromo people.

One day the Oromo people were offended by one of the Mijikenda. Two Oromo stuck their spears in the ground outside his hut, and waited for him inside. When the Mijikenda came home, he saw the two spears and got out his bow and arrow. As soon as he entered his hut, he surprised the two Oromo, and killed them both.

After this, Muyeye thought it would be a good idea to move his people away from the Oromo. He left Singwaya and stopped for a while at a small mountain called Mwangea. But the Oromo followed him there. The Mijikenda moved farther south to Mwaeba, but the Oromo still followed him. Finally, at a place called Kwa Demu, the Mijikenda were so numerous that they decided to split up into separate groups. Each group went in its own direction, and each people built its own *kaya* to protect it from the Oromo.

Most of the Mijikenda say that they first lived in a place called Singwaya, somewhere in southern Somalia. There are hundreds of traditions about Mijikenda origins. Each presents its own version of the migration into Kenya, but they do seem to show that they have common beginnings.

Historians believe the Mijikenda peoples

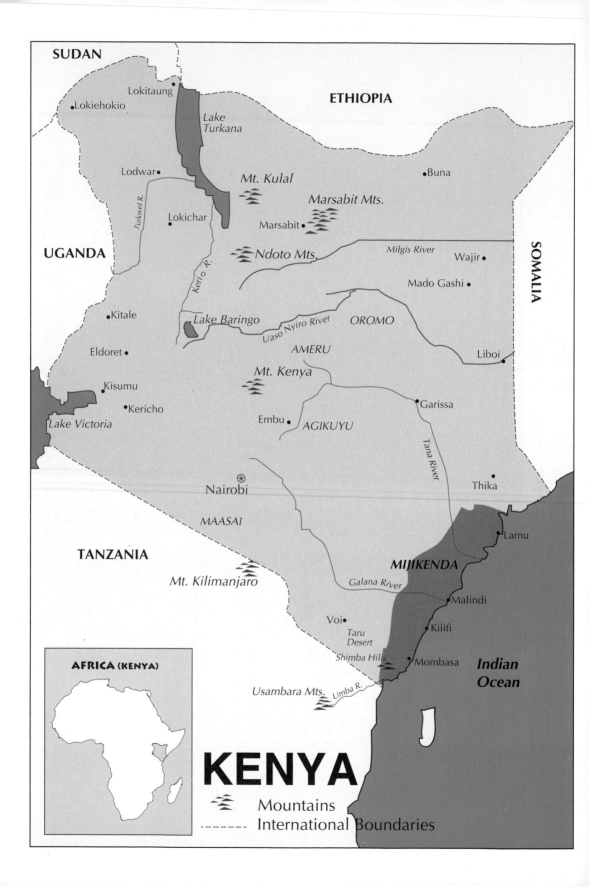

SUDAN

Lokitaung
•Lokiehokio

Lake
Turkana

ETHIOPIA

•Buna

Lodwar•

Mt. Kulal

Marsabit Mts.

Turkwel R.

•Lokichar

Marsabit•

Milgis River

Wajir•

SOMALIA

UGANDA

Kerio R.

Ndoto Mts.

Mado Gashi•

•Kitale

Lake Baringo

Uaso Nyiro River

OROMO

Liboi•

Eldoret•

AMERU

Kisumu•

Mt. Kenya

•Kericho

Lake Victoria

Embu•

AGIKUYU

Garissa•

Nairobi

Tana River

Thika•

MAASAI

Lamu•

TANZANIA

MIJIKENDA

Mt. Kilimanjaro

Galana River

Malindi•

Voi•

Kilifi•

AFRICA (KENYA)

Taru
Desert

Shimba Hills

Mombasa•

Indian
Ocean

Usambara Mts.

Umba R.

KENYA

Mountains

------- International Boundaries

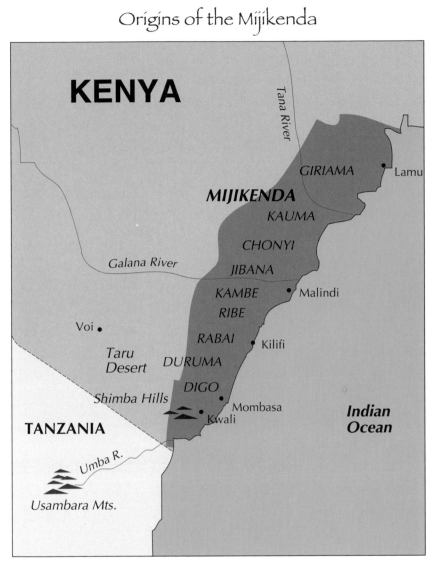

The Mijikenda traditionally live along the coast of Kenya.

migrated from southern Somalia because of conflicts with the Oromo people.

▼ THE LAND ▼

The Mijikenda live on the coast of Kenya in eastern Africa. They are spread over land

13

stretching 95 miles between the Sabaki River in
the north and Umba in the south. To the east,
on the coastal plain, live the Swahili. The
Oromo, Maasai, and Waata live in the Taru
desert to the west.

This land lies about 200 to 1,000 feet above
sea level, although the Shimba Hills are higher.
The land east of the hills is fairly green, but
farther west it becomes dry scrubland. Less than
a quarter of Mijikenda land is good for farming.

There are two rainy seasons. The short rains
come in October or November; the long rains,
in April or May. The rainfall varies from one
area to another. Some farmers can have a good
harvest while their neighbors have a crop failure.

Most Mijikenda live in their original home
areas, Kilifi and Kwale. Many can also be found
in the coastal cities of Mombasa and Malindi.▲

chapter

2

BEFORE AND AFTER THE *KAYA*

IN THE NINETEENTH CENTURY EACH MIJIKENDA group lived in a walled-in settlement called a *kaya*, which protected them against Oromo and Maasai attacks. The *kaya* was a large circular area on top of a hill, surrounded by dense forest. As population grew, new *makaya* (the plural of *kaya*) were built until there were twenty-four instead of the original nine. A *kaya* had two entrances, three gates, and a ritual symbol at the center.

Each *kaya* was divided into sections for the different *mbari* (clans). The Digo and Giriama had six clans; the Kauma and Kambe, five each; the Rabai, Ribe, Jibana, and Chonyi, four each; and the Duruma, three. As population grew, the clans were split into subclans and lineages. The lineages were made up of many *mriango*, or families, each named after its head.

A rural house constructed by the Mijikenda who live on or near the coast.

The clan was the basis of the Mijikenda social system. Clan members were expected to look after one another. If a person was accused of a crime and assessed a fine, his clan would help him pay it. Also, if a person won a case, he would share the payment he received with the elders of his clan.

Like many peoples of eastern Africa, the Mijikenda used a system of "age-sets" called *marika*. These were stages of life for boys, young men, and old men.

The most advanced and respected age-set

were the senior elders. They made important decisions for the *kaya* about politics, religion, and law. In difficult situations, they were assisted by the secret Vaya Society, made up of the most important elders.

Only members of the Vaya had power to use the Fisi, the magic oath whose name means "hyena." Oaths were regarded as solemn pacts with supernatural powers. They were used to protect property, to chase away evil spirits, or to hunt out people practicing witchcraft.

Besides the Vaya, the Giriama men had three other secret societies: the Habasi, Kinyenzi, and Gohu. People wishing to join these groups had to pay large fees. The women had their own society, called Kifudi. Men could join it, but could not take part in meetings or rituals.

The nine Mijikenda peoples sometimes met together to organize religious ceremonies, funerals, war, or trading caravans. Interaction between the many *makaya* was fairly common.

The Mijikenda survived mostly as farmers. The traditional crops were sorghum, millet, eulesine, and rice. The Mijikenda also grew beans, cassavas, sweet potatoes, pulses, yams, tomatoes, bananas, coconuts, and tobacco. Corn and palms became popular crops during the 19th century. The palms had many uses: From the meat came oil; wine was tapped from the shoots; baskets, mats, and roof shingles were

BLOOD-BROTHERHOOD

Long-distance trading was a dangerous business. In the nineteenth century, the traveling was done mostly on foot. Traders and their porters had all sorts of things to worry about: wild animals, enemy peoples, and thieves along the way. One way such traders protected themselves was by traveling in large groups, with armed guards. It was also helpful to make friends with the people who lived along the trade route.

A custom known as blood-brotherhood became very popular among trading communities. For example, a Giriama trader might form a blood-brotherhood with a Mkamba (member of the Akamba people). When the Giriama trader arrived in the land of the Akamba along his trade route, his Kamba blood-brother would take him into his home. There the Giriama would have protection and any help he needed. When the Kamba trader visited the coast, the Giriama brother would return the favor.

The blood-brotherhood pledge included not only the two men who made it, but also their families and clans. When the Akamba were struck by drought and famine in the 1820s, many of them went to the coast. The Kamba traders and their families lived with their Giriama blood-brothers there.

woven from the leaves, and the trunks were used as building materials.

Many Mijikenda families also kept goats, sheep, poultry, and cattle. Cattle-raising was especially important in the dry western lands of Mijikenda country. Hunting provided another source of food.

Craftsmen made objects that were both useful

Protected from the sun, these young sculptors carve figures that will be sold to tourists.

and beautiful. There were experts in pottery, basket-making, woodworking, clothmaking, and metal-working. The Giriama are especially famous for their wood sculptures.

Trade was an important part of the Mijikenda economy. The clans traded with each other and with neighboring peoples, especially the Swahili who lived in Mombasa on the coast. Mombasa traded cloth and jewelry for Mijikenda grain, ivory, rhinoceros horn, cattle, and hides.

During times of drought, the Mijikenda also received help from Mombasa, which brought grain in by ship. The Mijikenda often

sent their children to work for Mombasa families until the famine had passed. Sometimes, however, the children stayed. It was quite common for Mijikenda people to migrate to Mombasa for work, and then to become Swahili themselves.

The Mijikenda sent trade caravans inland to get some of the products they sold to Mombasa. Caravans began visiting the Chagga people, near Mount Kilimanjaro, and the Akamba near Mount Kenya.

In 1837 Mombasa underwent a change of government, and the Mijikenda lost much of their trading business. This new situation was part of the reason for a great change in the Mijikenda social system.

▼ LEAVING THE *KAYA* ▼

In the 1850s and '60s many Mijikenda decided to leave their traditional homes in search of new opportunities. There were several reasons for this.

After the civil war in Mombasa in 1837, the Mazrui, allies of the Mijikenda, moved from Mombasa to Takaungu, 35 miles to the north, on the coast. The Giriama, who were no longer trading much with Mombasa, followed the Mazrui. They began moving into Godama, a region near Takaungu. They set up successful farms and sold their products to Takaungu.

The Giriama felt safe in leaving their *kaya* because their traditional enemies, the Oromo and the Kwavi Maasai, had become less powerful. Both groups had been defeated in wars in the late 19th century. By the end of the 1890s the Mijikenda were scattered all over the area that they occupy today.

As cattle-raising became more important for some Mijikenda groups, more land was needed for grazing. Also, the population was growing. The lands around the original *makaya* were not large enough to meet these needs.

The resulting spreading out changed the role of the *kaya* in Mijikenda society. Gradually they came to be used only as sacred or ritual centers and symbols of unity for the various Mijikenda groups.

The elders lost much of their power to control trade and social behavior. The trade routes had moved, and younger men moved near the new routes. Without the elders' control, the younger men were freer to keep the profits from trading and to make decisions about their own marriages and businesses. It was now possible for young men to become wealthy.

The new communities had their own elders' councils to settle local conflicts. Regional councils were set up for larger areas. The elders also lost the power to divide land among the clans. In fact, the Mijikenda did not leave the

In past times, clans were an integral part of Mijikenda society. Today, emphasis is placed on individual achievement rather than that of the clan's.

makaya as clan groups, but as individuals. Thus the clans became less important in society.

It became difficult to organize ritual ceremonies that involved all the Mijikenda peoples. The age-set initiation ceremonies were shortened and held less often. In the 1870s a new age-set was supposed to be initiated, but only a few of the eligible men were able to attend the ritual. This was the last such ceremony organized by the Giriama.▲

chapter

3

CUSTOM AND RITUAL

BOTH DURING AND AFTER THE *KAYA* PERIOD, Mijikenda culture was marked by certain common ceremonies and beliefs.

As in most societies, marriage was important. A man had to choose a bride from a clan other than his own. He would visit a girl's father, bringing calabashes full of beer as a gift, and ask permission to marry his daughter. If the father approved, the young man had to pay a bridewealth or *mahunda* of six cows and a bull, or 65 goats.

If a Giriama couple did not get along, divorce was allowed. It was not common, however, partly because the father had to return the *mahunda*. The wife kept the children until they were grown, when they went to their father. He was expected to pay ten goats for them.

Digo women had more power in marriages.

A MIJIKENDA WEDDING

In a traditional Mijikenda wedding ceremony, there is much feasting and rejoicing. As in most cultures around the world, a wedding is a time to gather with friends, give gifts, and practice rituals that will bring good luck to the new couple.

The groom brings fifteen calabashes full of beer to the bride's father. These are thought to be payment for the children that the young couple will have. It is believed that if this payment were not made, the children would belong to the bride's father, not her husband.

On the night of the wedding, the bride is dressed in jewelry made of copper around her arms and neck. Then she is ready to attend the wedding feast. Neighbors come to join the festivities. A goat is slaughtered for the occasion, and all enjoy the feast. However, it is the custom for the men and the women to eat in separate groups.

After dinner, the bride undergoes a ritual to prepare her for her new life. One of the elder women of the *kaya* sprinkles her with fat from the goat slaughtered for the feast. Then the bride is wrapped in brightly colored cloth. She is given gourds of scented oils to take with her. She will use these oils as perfume.

Their clans were matrilinear, meaning that children belonged to the mother's clan, not the father's. The mother retained control of the children even after divorce.

Burial, like marriage, involved many rituals. The body was buried in a grave near the house where the dead person had lived. Woodcarvers made sculptures to celebrate the spirits of rich

VIGANGO: THE ART OF WOOD SCULPTURE

In traditional Mijikenda beliefs, the spirit of a person never dies, only the body. As with many African peoples, it is important to the Mijikenda to remember the spirits of people who have died. The Giriama have a custom of woodcarving meant for this purpose.

The Gohu was a society for very wealthy men. If a member of the Gohu died, his spirit would be remembered with a tall, thin woodcarving called a *kigango* (the plural is *vigango*). These were not gravestones. In fact, the graves of the dead were flattened in ritual dances, and were usually not marked. Instead, *vigango* would be placed near the homestead in a hut called *kigojo*. In this way the Giriama could pay respects to the spirits of important people in their community.

The *vigango* were made of the *muhuhu* tree, which is very hard wood that termites do not eat, so it lasts a long time. The logs were carved with complex patterns, usually using the triangle shape. They were colored black, white, and red. A wooden head was put on top, to represent the person but not to look real; they were usually flat, like a disc.

A *kigango* was made by specially trained woodworkers. Then a community ceremony took place. The *kigango* was the center of attention while ritual feasting, drinking, and praying took place. Around the tall *kigango* were placed small wooden pegs, decorated with colored ribbons. These sticks represented spirits who were not as important as the deceased Gohu.

elders. Less important people were remembered with small wooden pegs. Murder victims were buried outside the village fence.

An official mourning period began on the third day after a death. It lasted seven days for a man and six for a woman. The mourners sang, chanted, and danced. Food and beer were served. If the person had been murdered, a ceremony was held to purify the land.

The Mijikenda believed that a person's spirit, or *koma*, survived death. The *koma* had the same needs as a person. If a person died who was known to love beer, his son would pour a little beer on his grave every day for his *koma* to enjoy.

Other kinds of spirits, called *mapeho, mzuka,* or *mzimu,* were thought to be evil. Sometimes sacrifices were made to placate these spirits.

▼ RELIGION ▼

The Mijikenda believed in a supreme god, Mulungu. He was invoked on important occasions that affected all the peoples. For example, during a drought a rain ceremony was held around the *nyumba ya Mulungu* (house of god).

Some of the Mijikenda were influenced by Islam, which was followed by many of their Swahili neighbors on the coast. Some, especially among the Digo, actually converted to Islam.▲

chapter

4

THE EUROPEAN CONQUEST

MISSIONARIES WERE THE FIRST EUROPEANS TO meet the Mijikenda. The Mijikenda thought that they, and later European traders, were merely passing visitors. They were wrong. At the time, Europe was already planning how to conquer and divide Africa.

By 1895 Britain had control over Kenya, which they called the East African Protectorate. The Mazrui Swahili rebelled against the new colonial government. Many of the peoples on the coast, especially the Giriama, came to their aid, providing them with food supplies and information on the whereabouts of the British.

The British used threats and bribery to keep the Giriama from helping the Mazrui rebels, and some Giriama elders cooperated. The Mazrui war with the British ended in 1896.

To attract European settlers, the colonial

The Mijikenda established themselves at the center of the coastal trade.

authorities seized large pieces of land in central
Kenya, especially from the Maasai and the
Agikuyu. This move also was a way to obtain
labor from the dispossessed Africans. In addi-
tion, Africans were charged taxes. In order to pay
these, they either had to sell produce or earn wages.

Along the coastal region, colonial interests

The Mijikenda are expert builders of large boats called *dhows*, skills learned from Arabs that colonized the coast long ago. The *dhow* can carry up to 50 tons.

soon clashed with the Mijikenda. The colonial authorities were impressed by the richness of the Sabaki valley and the coastal lowlands. They decided to seize 100,000 acres of Giriama land north of the Sabaki River.

At the time the Mijikenda were also moving into the lush coastal lowlands, which formerly were owned by Arabs and Swahili. The Mijikenda prospered there. The other coastal peoples became more dependent than ever on Mijikenda grain and palm products.

The Mijikenda were once again at the center of coastal trade. They were able to provide work for large numbers of former slaves. Some local officials were impressed by the Mijikenda's hard work and success, but the colonial authorities in Mombasa had other ideas. The British invented a rumor that the Mijikenda were drunks and lazy, and they used it to try to destroy the Mijikenda economy and turn this people into a class of laborers.

The number of European plantations and companies at the coast increased steadily, but they all suffered from labor shortages. They managed to recruit some workers from central and western Kenya, but they wanted a more reliable and cheaper local labor force.

The working conditions, however, were too horrible to attract local workers. Being used to the city, few Swahili were willing to work on European farms. The former slaves were willing, but there were not enough of them. That left the Mijikenda, the largest native population in the area. But with their own successful farming and trade economy, the Mijikenda were not interested in working for the Europeans.

Therefore the British turned to force, seizing more Mijikenda land. The Giriama were the first to be targeted because they were the largest and

most successful of the Mijikenda people. In 1908 a boundary was established separating the Giriama from the Swahili and Arabs.

When the British had taken control of Kenya, they had appointed headmen to carry out colonial duties in each community. In 1913, pressure was put on Giriama headmen to find more workers and collect more taxes. The headmen were not the most senior elders in the Mijikenda age-set system; therefore they did not command respect. The Giriama did all they could to avoid paying taxes. Some moved to distant places, others lied about their age. Some even attacked the tax collectors.

Next the Giriama were ordered to leave their northern coastal lands called the Trans-Sabaki for a "native reserve" near Malindi. The Giriama resistance grew rapidly and soon found a leader in a remarkable woman named Mekatili.

The British threatened to send the army to end Giriama resistance. They arrested or publicly insulted Giriama leaders. But this only made the Giriama less willing to cooperate. When they refused to leave Trans-Sabaki on October 1 as ordered, the colonial government moved them by armed patrols, burned their houses, and destroyed their property.

The outbreak of World War I made the British more determined to force the Giriama into their service. On August 17 British-Giriama hostility

The Mijikenda retained a fierce independence in the face of British rule.

exploded into open conflict after a policeman raped a Giriama woman.

Both sides prepared for war, but it was an unequal contest. The colonial troops marched

MEKATILI AND THE GIRIAMA REBELLION

In June 1913, the Provincial Commissioner addressed a public meeting. He urged the Giriama to pay taxes, obey colonial laws, and above all to send their young men to work for the Europeans. Many in the audience did not like what they heard. Among them was Mekatili, a bright woman with a gift for public speaking.

A few days later she called the women from her area to a meeting in her home. She spoke of the evils of British rule. Their sons were being taken away, she said, and many never returned. Their daughters, too, were marrying strangers and many also never returned. The women agreed that something had to be done. Mekatili's message and following began to spread.

At first the British did not take her seriously. They soon discovered how wrong they were. Mekatili won the support of the most respected Giriama male elders, Ngonyo and Wanje. She openly called the headmen traitors to their people. She demanded that Giriama become independent once again. People were encouraged to visit the *kaya* and speak to the elders about their situation, and to practice traditional Giriama rituals.

At the *kaya* oaths were taken to unite against the British and bring back traditional Giriama government and customs; the effects were soon to be seen. The Giriama stopped working for the Europeans, no one paid taxes, and even headmen stopped meeting in councils. Angry and frustrated, the British arrested Mekatili on October 17. A few days later the elder, Wanje, was also arrested.

Imprisoned in western Kenya, in April 1914 they escaped and returned to Giriama. The British captured them again in early August. But by that time the Giriama were ready for open rebellion against colonial rule.

The lifestyle of the Mijikenda involves fishing, farming, and raising animals.

through Giriama territory, burning villages, looting livestock, and firing on the people. The Giriama finally sued for peace, but their request was not accepted. The colonial government was determined to crush Giriama independence.

It was not until October 1914 that the government agreed to end the conflict. By then the war with Germany was going badly, and the British troops were needed elsewhere. But their decision made things worse for the Giriama. They were obliged to pay a fine of 100,000 rupees, provide 1,000 men to serve as porters in the war—and they still had to leave Trans-Sabaki.▲

chapter

5

CHANGES CAUSED BY COLONIAL RULE

LIFE WAS HARD FOR THE GIRIAMA IN THE years following the rebellion. They had to pay the huge fine, leave the fertile Trans-Sabaki region to go to the overcrowded reserve, and become laborers for the British. Actually, more Giriama became workers than the British had required. The government took this to mean that they were becoming more tractable; in truth, however, the Giriama were becoming poorer and desperately needed work.

By 1916, partly because of the fine and partly because of a drought, famine broke out. The Giriama remember it as *nzala ya faini*, "the famine of the fine." Forced to change their tactics, from 1918 the British allowed them to resume farming the Trans-Sabaki. The colonial authorities concluded that this was better than famine and rebellion. They were finally realizing

A Mijikenda gathering cultivated coconuts.

that the Giriama were not going to be turned into a working class.

But the local authorities still wanted control of Giriama and other Mijikenda territory. Many of the British-appointed headmen had grown old or disrespected. The Giriama wanted good leadership that would look out for their own interests.

Thus both the British and the Giriama decided to revive the traditional Giriama government. They wanted to establish a new *kambi* or council of elders, but no one knew how to go about it. There was only one person alive, Wanje, who had taken part in such a ceremony in 1870. It was doubtful that he would remember all the details. Morever, the *kaya* where the ceremony should have been held had been destroyed.

But they kept trying. Kaya Giriama was reopened, and Wanje and Mekatili went to live there. Wanje was made head of the *kambi*, and Mekatili headed the women's *kambi*, but the two held no positions in the government. In fact, this is as far as matters went. Official ceremonies for the new council were never held.

Mijikenda trade was affected by colonial government decisions. In efforts to force the Mijikenda to become laborers, the British tried to prevent them from using their trade routes. Instead, a few closely controlled trading centers

The game of bao is a popular pastime for many people in East Africa. It is quick and interesting, involving complex mathematical calculations.

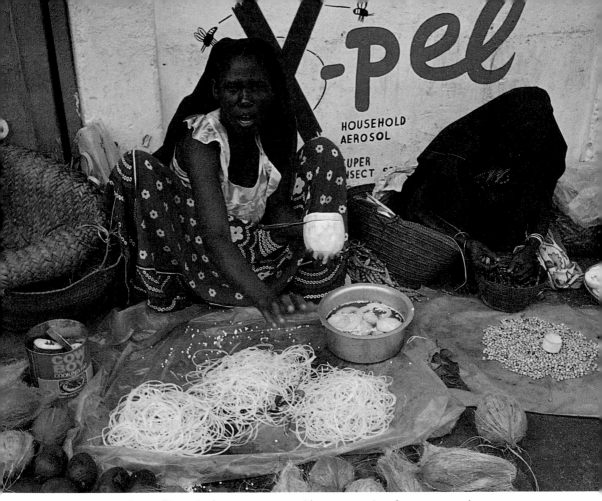

A vendor selling whole coconuts and long strands of coconut pulp.

were established. Because transportation was poor, many Mijikenda could not use these centers. They were no longer trading with their old allies, the Arabs and Swahili. Instead they had to deal with new traders, mostly from India, who were interested only in making a profit, not friendships. Many rural farmers came to owe money to these traders.

Tax collection time was right after the harvest. To get money, the Mijikenda had to sell their crops at a time when they could not get good prices for them. Many ended up selling most of their grain, and then had to buy it back at high prices when they ran out.

All over Kenya, people who had lost their land worked on someone else's land in exchange for being able to use a piece of the land themselves. The Mijikenda were not allowed to own land outside their overcrowded, arid "Nyika Reserve." Those who moved out of the reserve to the coastal lowlands became squatters of Arab-Swahili landowners.

As squatters, the Mijikenda were not guaranteed the right to stay on the land. Therefore they did not plant profitable crops that took several years to produce, such as coconut palms. On the other hand, the landowners had little control over the squatters. They could not force them to work long hours because they were neither slaves or paid laborers. Thus neither the squatters nor the landlords worked the land fully, and the economy on the coast could not improve.

Many Mijikenda workers preferred to be casual laborers instead of registered workers. This permitted them to switch jobs from day to day and work only when they needed to. They could also earn money in other ways, such as farming, and they could live in their own villages, avoiding the terrible living conditions of the working class in the city.

The colonial era was a period of rapid social

change. Growing numbers of Mijikenda converted to Islam. Because many Mijikenda became squatters on Arab and Swahili land, they often converted to Islam as a way to be accepted into the Swahili community. Some even came to be thought of as Swahili themselves.

Christianity and mission schools were not popular. Connected with the colonial government, they were not trusted.

In the meantime, Muslim or Koranic schools, known as *madrassa*, were very popular. These schools were based on the beliefs of Islam. Sometimes Koranic schools competed directly with colonial schools. In the early 1920s, for example, Digo Muslims at Waa built a *madrassa* next to a government school. The colonial school was forced to close and move to Mombasa.

In the next two decades school enrollment for Mijikenda children was very low. Some progress was made in the 1950s, when school enrollment grew closer to the national average in Kenya. Although Koranic schools were the most popular, they taught skills that were not highly valued in colonial Kenyan society. This left the Mijikenda at a disadvantage.▲

chapter

6

THE MIJIKENDA AND INDEPENDENCE

IN THE DECADES FOLLOWING THE GIRIAMA rebellion against colonial rule, anticolonial protest spread and grew stronger in other parts of Kenya. The most extreme and violent movement was called Mau Mau. In 1963 the British were eventually forced to grant the peoples of Kenya their independence.

After the Giriama Rebellion, the educated Mijikenda formed political groups to help the interests of their people. The earliest was the Young Nyika Association, formed in 1931. It called for the Mijikenda to be given more and fertile land, among other things.

Mijikenda politics entered a new era during and after World War II. The war brought many hardships. People who joined the army were promised many things, including land and better jobs. But when they returned, none of these

were given to them. They also came back with changed views. They had met people from other parts of the colonial world and learned of their struggles for independence.

It was because of these new views that the Digo Welfare Association, the Young Duruma Association, and the Mijikenda Union were formed in 1945, and the Rabai Welfare Association in 1946. The main objective of the Mijikenda Union was to unite and promote the progress of the Mijikenda as a whole rather than as separate groups.

The colonial authorities opposed the Mijikenda Union, which spoke out against unpopular colonial chiefs and other aspects of government policy, especially over land. In the meantime, the nationwide Kenya African Union, formed in 1944, spread its activities to the coast.

The political tensions that had been brewing in Kenya finally blew up in the early 1950s. At that time the Mau Mau war erupted, and the government declared a state of emergency. The war was fought mainly in central Kenya, but its effects were also felt on the coast. As Kenya's independence seemed more likely, new political parties were founded. They represented the interests of the major coastal groups: the Swahili, the Arabs, and the Mijikenda.

The most famous Mijikenda politician in the 1950s and 1960s was Ronald Ngala. Trained in mission schools, he became a teacher. Although he was a Christian and wanted to modernize his society, he was interested in Mijikenda tradition. Before a major campaign Ngala always went to the *kaya* to be blessed by the elders.

In 1957 Ngala was one of fourteen Africans to win a seat in the first elections held for the colonial legislative council. Ngala soon proved his leadership qualities. In 1960 he led talks in London to establish Kenyan independence. He then became the leader of the Kenyan African Democratic Union, a new political party. After independence he was made a senior minister and a vice-president of the Kenyan African National Union. His son, Katana Ngala, became a major politician in the 1980s.

After independence, the lot of the Mijikenda was better, as it was for many other Kenyan communities. For example, the number of children who went to school in the Mijikenda districts for Kwale and Kilifi nearly doubled in the first ten years of independence and almost doubled again between 1974 and 1984.

The provision of roads, health, and water facilities to Mijikenda areas improved as well. Kwale District was one of the fourteen divisions chosen for the Special Rural Development Program launched in the late 1960s. The program aimed at improving the rural roads, water

By 1948 many Mijikenda had moved to cities like Mombasa to find work for wages.

supply, education, and health. It also taught new farming methods.

Farmers began to grow more cash crops, grown to be sold for money, not to be eaten or used by the farmers themselves. In this way the farmers stimulated the economy and had more money.

Although they were advancing, however, the Mijikenda still lagged behind other ethnic groups in Kenya.▲

chapter

7

CHANGES NOW AND INTO THE FUTURE

THE DEVELOPMENTS THAT WERE BROUGHT BY independence caused other important changes among the Mijikenda. In the 1970s and 1980s the coastal population grew rapidly. Change has also taken place in the social system. Different social classes can now be seen in the rural areas. There are traders, and there are farmers. The farmers themselves are divided according to the amount of land they have and the crops they grow.

The rich farmers own large tracts of land and grow mainly cash crops, especially palms from which copra is produced. Copra is the meat of the palm, the source of the oil. Many farmers began growing copra because prices for it nearly tripled between 1950 and 1967. Some of these farmers are now also involved in commerce and trucking.

Historic monument, Fort Jesus, constructed by Portuguese colonists during the 1500s. It was subsequently conquered by the Arabs, reconquered by the Portuguese, and finally by English colonists.

The work on farms is not handled the way it used to be. The communal work group has changed. Among the Digo, for example, in the past a person could ask his neighbors for help so long as he could feed them. This was called *wiri*. Or a small group of families could take turns working on each other's farms without supplying food. This was called *kukumbana*.

Now people with little or no land are forced to hire themselves out as laborers for the farmers who can afford to hire extra help. The poorer farmers have to depend of family help.

The new Kenyan government encouraged the

sale of land to individuals, not a traditional practice for most Kenyan peoples. The government
believed that private ownership would be good
for the future of agriculture. They tended to ask
the older heads of homesteads to tell them who
had rights to what land. This increased the
power of the older men over the younger men,
resulting in greater generational conflicts. Also,
the land was mostly sold to men, not women.
This became a problem among matrilinear
groups such as the Digo, who traditionally
passed land from mother to child.

The government also encouraged people to
start cattle ranches in the western cattle-rearing
areas. Ranching, it was thought, would improve
the care of the animals and protect grazing lands
from traditional herding methods that were
thought to be destructive. By the mid-1980s,
however, these ranches were hardly successful.

As private land ownership became common,
the land was often sold to outsiders. Many
Mijikenda are unhappy that people from other
parts of Kenya and from abroad have been buy-
ing land at the coast. Land disputes between the
Mijikenda and outsiders have been intensifying.

Noticeable changes have also occurred in
marriage customs. Many of them concern the
bridewealth. Formerly a certain number of
cattle, today it is often in cash. The cost of the
bridewealth has also risen. This is partly because

of the rising cost of living, but also because fathers have been demanding a greater bridewealth for more educated daughters. It has also become common to expect the bridewealth to be paid in a short time. Stretching out livestock payments made sense, but stretching out payments of money does not.

Another change in marriage customs is that men now have more power over their wives and children. It is somewhat harder for a woman to get a divorce because her father would have to pay the bridewealth back in cash.

The changes in marriage practices are most clearly seen among the Digo. Traditionally the women had some power in Digo marriages, since this society was matrilinear. Now there is a new form of marriage called *harusi chidzomba*, under which husbands have many rights over their wives and children. This custom was influenced by Islam and shows the growing power of the patrilinear system.

The influence of Islam can also be seen in ritual practices. Mijikenda groups that at first resisted Islam, such as the Giriama, have been adopting more and more Islamic practices and rituals. Diviners and specialists in herbal medicines now combine the new Islamic rituals with traditional Mijikenda ones. Wealthy businessmen sometimes use Islamic ritual prohibitions to excuse themselves from Mijikenda ceremonies

A Mijikenda woman wearing traditional Islamic dress.

Children of Mijikenda-Arab decent at play.

at which they would normally be expected to spend money on food and drink.

The change to Islam in Giriama society can be seen in the trading center called Kaloleni. This small place was connected by paved road to Mombasa in 1975, and electricity and water were added. Businesses there grew, and along with them the Muslim population. In 1978 an elegant mosque was built, and an even larger one added in the mid-1980s. By that time it was common for the Giriama to give Swahili names to their non-Muslim children. The parents believed that the Islamic spirits wanted it that way.

The power of Islamic spirits also was clear among women. Sometimes women became possessed by spirits. When they were believed possessed, these women were feared and respected. In this way they could win freedom from the restrictions of society. A Mijikenda woman who had converted to Islam had more rights than other women because she was somewhat feared.

By the mid-1980s some 40 percent of the Mijikenda were Muslim, another 40 percent followed their traditional religions, and the rest belonged to Christian churches. Compared to other Kenyan peoples, such as the Agikuyu, Akamba, and Luo, there are still very few Christians among the Mijikenda.

The government takes a keen interest in religious and ritual matters. It has particularly been interested to root out spirit possession dances and belief in witchcraft, beliefs that are thought to keep the society "backward." In the 1960s and 1970s a diviner and herbalist named Kajiwe was encouraged to sweep through Mijikenda country to hunt out witches and bring an end to witchcraft. It is difficult to say whether or not he succeeded in his mission, but he did become very wealthy in the process.

From the early 1970s the government also encouraged traditional herbalists to become more professional and form medical associations. Among the associations formed were the Jami-Tiba Society of East Africa and the Miti ya

One type of traditional hairstyle worn by the Mijikenda.

Shamba. Also, in 1975 diviners and herbalists were required to be licensed to practice.

Some Mijikenda are disturbed by these societal changes. They have occurred mostly in the areas nearest to the coast, where the mixture of peoples and cultures is greatest. This has led the Giriama, for example, to call the coast in the east "modern" and the western inland areas "traditional."

People living in the less crowded west are thought to be closer to Mijikenda traditions and customs. They live in larger homesteads surrounded by relatives and are believed to

On the coast it was traditional for elders to smoke the waterpipe.

share more, prefer traditional dress, and celebrate the spirits of the ancestors. In contrast, people in the densely populated east are believed to be ambitious, greedy for land and money, and too eager to adopt the customs, dress, and mannerisms of foreigners.

Part of the Giriama's view of the west as more traditional is because it is the site of their original *kaya*. It reminds them of their cultural identity in a period of rapid social and cultural change. The *kaya* has come to be seen as a sacred place, the center of Giriama knowledge and tradition.

As late as 1988 the *kaya* elders organized rain-making ceremonies. At that time there was a terrible drought in the region. The elders performed rituals to purify the land and prayed for rain and the fertility of the soil. Within days it rained. This greatly helped the public image of the traditional *kaya* elders.

But there is no question that the Mijikenda live in a world different from that of their fathers and forefathers. Traditional social groupings such as clans and age-sets have lost most of their functions and meaning. In the early 1980s only three quarters of the Mijikenda were aware of which clan they belonged to. Less than a quarter of them belonged to age-sets.▲

CONCLUSION

THE HISTORY OF THE MIJIKENDA CLEARLY demonstrates that the formation of ethnic groups is a complex and ongoing process. The nine peoples of the Mijikenda have certain strong differences in their cultures. Some have traditions of origin from the south. Some believe their ancestors came from the north. Some of the Mijikenda in the south have matrilinear traditions. The male-dominated traditions of the other Mijikenda and the Islamic world are meeting those traditions and conflicting with them.

In spite of these differences, the Mijikenda see themselves in many ways as a unified group. Ever since they left their traditional *makaya* in the nineteenth century to spread along the coast of Kenya, the Mijikenda have experienced many changes and challenges as a people.

Today the Mijikenda are more numerous and

Although many traditions have been lost, the Mijikenda sense of culture and heritage is still very strong.

more diverse than ever. They are losing many of their traditions as they further integrate into Kenyan society. The Mijikenda struggle to balance the demands of modernization and traditional culture.▲

Glossary

Chonyi One of the peoples of the Mijikenda.
Digo One of the peoples of the Mijikenda.
Durama One of the peoples of the Mijikenda.
Giriama One of the peoples of the Mijikenda.
harusi chidzomba Digo form of marriage.
Jibana One of the peoples of the Mijikenda.
Kambe One of the peoples of the Mijikenda.
kambi Council of elders.
Kauma One of the peoples of the Mijikenda.
kaya (pl. *makaya*) Hilltop settlement of a
   Mijikenda people.
kigango Woodcarving in honor of the spirit of a
   dead person.
koma Spirit of a dead person.
mahuda Bridewealth among the Mijikenda.
mbari Clan.
mrianjo Mijikenda family.
Rabai One of the peoples of the Mijikenda.
Ribe One of the peoples of the Mijikenda.
Sabaki Language group of the Mijikenda
   peoples.

For Further Reading

Berg-Schlosser, Dirk. *Traditions and Change in Kenya*. Munich: Ferdinand Schoningh, 1984.

Brantley, Cynthia. *The Giriama and Colonial Resistance in Kenya, 1800–1920*. Berkeley: University of California Press, 1981.

Champion, Arthur M. *The Agiryama of Kenya*. Edited by John Middleton. London: Royal Anthropological Institute, 1967.

Krapf, Ludwig. *A Nika-English Dictionary*. London: Society for Promoting Christian Knowledge, 1887.

Parkin, David J. *Palms, Wine, and Witnesses*. San Francisco: Chandler Publishing, 1972.

———. *Sacred Void: Spatial Images of Work and Ritual Among the Giriama of Kenya*. Cambridge, England: Cambridge University Press, 1991.

Prins, Adriaan Hendrik Johan. *The Coastal Tribes of the North-Eastern Bantu*. London: International African Institute, 1952.

Slater, Mariam. *African Odyssey: An Anthropological Adventure*. Garden City, NY: Anchor, 1978.

Spear, Thomas. *The Kaya Complex: A History of the Mijikenda Peoples of Kenya Coast to 1900.* Athens: Ohio University Center for International Studies, Africa Program, 1978.

————. *Traditions of Origin and Their Interpretation: The Mijikenda of Kenya.* Athens: Ohio University Center for International Studies, Africa Program, 1982.

Willis, Justin. *Mombasa, the Swahili, and the Making of the Mijikenda.* Oxford: Clarendon, 1993.

Wolfe, Ernie. *Vigango: The Commemorative Sculpture of the Mijikenda of Kenya.* Williamstown, MA: Williams College Museum of Art, 1986.

Index

A
Agikuyu, 28, 52
Akamba, 18, 20, 52

B
basket-making, 19
blood-brotherhood, 18
British rule, 27–34
burial, 24

C
cattle-raising, 18, 21, 48
Chonyi (group), 9, 15
Christianity, 41, 52
clans, decline of, 21–22
clothmaking, 19
copra, 46
Council, regional, 21
crafts, 18–19
criminal justice, 16

D
Digo (group), 9, 15, 23, 24,
    26, 41, 47–48

diviner, 49, 52–53
divorce, 23–24, 49
drought, 19–20, 26, 35, 55
Duruma (group), 9, 15

E
elders, 17, 21

F
famine, 20
farming, 17, 46–48
Fisi (magic oath), 17

G
Giriama (group), 9, 15, 17,
    18–19, 20–22, 27,
    49–55
  rebellion against British,
    31–34, 42

H
harusi chidzomba (marriage
    form), 49
herbalists, 49, 52–53

hunting, 18

I

independence, Kenyan,
42–45
Islam, 26, 41, 49, 51–52

J

Jibana (group), 9, 15

K

Kaloleni, 51
Kamba (group), 9, 15
kambi (council of elders), 37
Kauma (group), 9, 15
kaya (plural, *makaya*;
hilltop), 15, 17,
20–22, 33, 37, 55
Kifudi (women's society), 17
kigango (woodcarving), 25
Kilifi (region), 14, 44–45
koma (human spirit), 26
kukumbana (family
cooperation), 47
Kwale (region), 14, 44–45

L

land, seizure of, 28–29, 30
language
Bantu family, 9
Pokomo, 10
Sabaki, 9
Swahili, 10

M

Maasai, 14, 15, 21, 28

madrassa (Koranic schools),
41
mahunda (bridewealth), 23,
48–49
Malindi, 14, 31
mapeho (evil spirit), 26
marika (age-set), 16, 22, 31,
55
marriage customs, 23, 48
Mau Mau, 42, 43
Mazrui, 20, 27
mbari (clans), 15, 16, 21, 55
matrilinear, 24, 48, 49
patrilinear, 49
Mbodze, Matsezi (first
Giriama women), 11
Mekatili (Giriama woman
leader), 31, 37
metal-working, 19
missions, Christian, 27, 41
Mombasa, 14, 19–20, 45,
51
mourning, 26
mriango (family), 15
muhuhu tree, 25
Mulungu (deity), 26
murder, 26
Muyeye (first Giriama man)
mzimu (evil spirit), 26
mzuka (evil spirit), 26

N

Ngala, Katana, 44
Ngala, Ronald, 43–44
Nyika (Nika) (bush people),
9

Nyika reserve, 35, 40
nyumba ya Mulungu (house
    of god), 26
nzala ya faina (famine of the
    fine), 35

O
origin, myth of, 11
Oromo, 12, 14, 15, 21

P
palm trees, 17–18, 46
political action, Mijikenda,
    43–45
pottery, 19

R
Rabai (group), 9, 15
rain ceremony, 26
rainfall, 14
Ribe (group), 9, 15

S
Sabaki River, 9, 12, 29
Singwaya, 11
Somalia, migration from,
    10–11

squatters, 40, 41
Swahili, 19, 30, 51

T
taxes, British-assessed, 28,
    31
trade, 18, 19, 30, 37–39, 46
Trans-Sabaki region 29–34,
    35

V
Vaya Society, 17

W
Waata, 14
Wanje (Giriama elder), 33
    37
wedding ceremony, 24
wiri (farm help), 47
witchcraft, 52
women (Digo) and marriage,
    23
wood sculpture, 19, 24, 25

Y
Young Nyika Association, 42

ABOUT THE AUTHOR

Tiyambe Zeleza was born in Harare, Zimbabwe, and grew up in Malawi. He received a master's degree at the University of London and a Ph.D. in history at Dalhousie University, Halifax, Nova Scotia. He has studied and taught at universities around the world. He is currently an associate professor of history at Trent University, Peterborough, Ontario.

Dr. Zeleza is the author of two works of fiction and several historical works, including *A Modern Economic History of Africa: The Nineteenth Century*. He is coauthor of the four-volume *Themes in Kenyan and World History*.

ABOUT THE AUTHOR: Jennifer Croft
ABOUT THE AUTHOR: Kim Sonsky